The Last Rose

By Curtis D. Ward

Atria Book Publishing
USA

Atria Book Publishing
USA

Copyright © 2010 Curtis D. Ward
All rights reserved.

No part of this book may be reproduced, stored in a retrieval system, or transmitted by any means, except for brief quotations in printed reviews, without the written permission of the author.

ISBN: 978-1-61240-002-0

First published by Atria Book Publishing
October 2010.

Printed in the United States of America.

Further information is contained
in the back matter of this book.

Dedication

To the love of my life—Rebecca.

From the moment our eyes first met you have never failed to captivate me. You are my passion, my companion, my lover, my friend, and the one with whom I choose to spend my life.

You gave me two wonderful children and as we traveled abroad you assisted me in birthing more souls into the Kingdom. Without you I am incomplete. Without you the brilliancy of life fades to gray.

It is for you I have put this book together. Your very essence is the poetry of my soul and the very inspiration that flows from my pen. It was for you I pulled many of these words from the depth of my spirit and penned them to common paper.

It was for you that I have loved, lived, and hoped for the future.

In a world full of dismal entropy, when all seemed despair, I found your love—like the last rose of summer.

I love you Angel Girl.

Contents

Dedication. iii
Preface..vii
Acknowledgments..viii

I Poetry..xi
The Last Rose...1
The Meadow...3
On Crimson Wings..4
Lovers Leap..6
Rose..7
The Sheep..9
The Portrait..11
The Chosen Angel 13
Unstoppable...14
I Refuse to Say Goodbye..15
It is Night...17
The Return...18
Ocean Talk...19
Just Close Your Eyes...22
The Broken Fiddle...24
When My Season Comes..26
Leaves That Were Green..27
Dad or Fool..28
The Hero 29
Meditation..31
Both Day and Night..32
The Stolen Rose..33
Sand...36
In the Palm..38

II Poetry of the Surreal..41
The Ghost of Orange...43
The Crimson Wolf..46

The Jester..47
The Woman of My Dreams...49

III Little Songs of Love..51
Beckyville..53
My Little AngelGirl..54

IV Collected Poetry..55
The Elder's Song...57
Time..59
Woolyburger Hill..60

V Essays and Prose..61
The Old Guitar..63
Grandma..66
The Kiss I Never Gave Her...67
Sign of a Miracle...70
A Trip to Remember..76
Yesterday...96
Observing an Orange..98
A Drive Through the City..99
True Love...101

Preface

This book contains poetry and prose written from 1969 to 2010. This is not all of the poetry and prose written during those years, but it is a good representation of my writings during that time period. They cover a very wide and diverse range of subjects. From lofty words uttered in a garden of roses to the darkness of despair at Lover's Leap, from the inner struggles of man's inner madness to the joy of celebrating faith in God—I have written something that will hopefully connect with you in some way.

This book is divided into five sections. Section one (I Poetry) consists of poetry written by myself. Section two (II Poetry of the Surreal) consists of poetry I have written in the past which is of a surreal nature. In section three (III Little Songs of Love) are portions of songs written by myself for Rebecca when we first met. Section number four (IV Collected Poetry) contains poetry written by my wife Rebecca, my son Brandon, and my daughter Makayla. Section number five (V Essays and Prose) contain short essays I have written throughout the years. Some were written and privately stuffed away in my files and some were written while in college.

With the exception of the three poems in section four, every poem and every word of prose was written by myself. I alone take responsibility for any errors or inadequacies.

I hope the numerous references to the "rose" or "roses" are not redundant, however the rose has been a reoccurring theme in the three and a half decade romance with my precious wife.

May the words in this book dance in your heart and rest in your soul. May you find some measure of hope, self reflection, or enjoyment in them.

Acknowledgments

I would like to acknowledge all of the individuals who have influenced my life and writing throughout the years: Rebecca Ward, the love of my life, my great inspiration, and the poetry of my soul; Professor Diane Kinser, my English 101 teacher who watered my potential as a writer and poet and influenced me beyond words. Thank you Diane. I will forever be grateful to you; Dr. Deveonne Tyree Cooke PsyD, my long time friend and colleague, for her support and constant encouragement; Mrs. Kathleen Withers, my elementary fourth grade teacher who whetted my sluggish appetite to read by informing me that she didn't care what I read, just as long as I read. It was her supply of Spiderman and Superman comic books that eventually led me to Shakespeare and Robert Frost. Thank you, oh noble teacher, may your precious soul rest in peace; Ada Kennedy, the very brilliant and colorful, not to mention a bit eccentric, English literature teacher who during my junior high school years lavished me with various pieces of prose and poetry and so highly praised my own feeble attempts at writing poetry myself. I can still hear your generous words of praise and encouragement; Mr. Robertson, my high school English teacher who instilled in me, rather true or no, that I was a writer and poet with a very special gift. You believed in me when I did not believe in myself. You will never know how you changed the course of my life; Florence Woods, my grandmother, who fed me a constant supply of books to feed my hungry spirit and encouraged me to seek the quiet time to engulf myself in them; The Alexander High School Spartan Press for my very first published poem "It is Night" in 1969; My home church and the pastors that nurtured and taught me to turn my words over to divine inspiration; The many people whom I have never been privileged to personally know but who greatly influenced my writing: Bob Dylan, thank you for showing me, when I was just a teenager, that poetry was "cool"; Simon & Garfunkel, thank you for words that danced through the atmosphere like a scented tapestry of parsley, sage, rosemary and thyme; Chris Rice, I will be forever grateful for your poetic lyrics which cause the deep to "calleth unto deep"; Robert Frost whose words of poetry have fed me, revived me, and painted pictures within my inner soul making this bleak world a more beautiful place to pass through; William Shakespeare, whose brilliant understanding of human nature and command of the English language is still not fully realized by many; William Tyndale, the one man who single handedly took the English language out of the hands of hacks and painted it within the spirits of writers and poets for generations to come. No man has contributed more beauty in words, phrases, and speech than this one man. It has been rightly said that without a William Tyndale there never would have been a William Shakespeare. Thank you for that great English work of art you so willingly gave your life for by being burned at the stake—the English translation of the Bible. Ninety percent of the New Testament, and almost seventy five percent of the Old Testament, of the King James Version of the English Bible was carried over directly from the translation penned by the gifted, silver tongued William Tyndale—the true master of inspired English prose and poetry; Dickinson, Wordsworth, Blake, Whitman, Longfellow, and a host of others too numerous to mention—you gave life to words.

Last but certainly not least, the four greatest inspirations of my life; The Lord Jesus Christ who changed the life of a disgruntled hippy poet into one of great joy and purposeful living, and revealed to me the ultimate purpose and the great mystery of existence; Ramona Jill Ward, my precious mother, who raised me to believe I could do the impossible and didn't stop believing for me until I believed it for myself; Janet Settle, my beloved mother-in-law, whose constant praise of my literary work encouraged me beyond words; Rebecca Ward, my wonderful wife, for whom much of my poetry and this very book was written. I mention you again . . . and again . . . and again. Thank you for laboring over the cover and and other details with me and for your unending support. You have encouraged me and moved me and I love you. You are the inspiration for the poetry of my soul. It was for you I pulled many of these words from the depth of my spirit and put them to print. It was for you that I have loved, lived, and hoped for the future. When it seemed I was walking through this dismal world alone, I found your love—like the last rose of summer.

I would like to also acknowledge others who made this immediate book possible: Louis and Jan Settle for backing this project; My sister Tammy and brother-in-law Bob, for assisting me; Kimberly Hjelt for her invaluable suggestions; Harry Pratt Judson, LLD. and Ida C. Bender, *Graded Literature Readers* (Maynard, Merrill, and Co., 1899) for the beautiful image of the rose and the University of South Florida for allowing me to use it on the Dedication page; Freesurf for the front cover design and Tolchik for the back cover design, (although I did alter both); My family, Rebecca, Brandon, and Makayla, not only for allowing me to submit their beautiful poetry but for putting up with my endless hours, weeks, and months at the keyboard and multiple tasks I left unfinished while compiling and writing the manuscript for this book.

I
Poetry

The Last Rose

Green leaves of summer have turned to brown,
twirling and tumbling to the ground.
An autumn breeze makes the town aware
a cold hint of winter is in the air.

The boys have made their swimming hole
just a place to take their fishing pole.
Hopscotch is not played on the walk,
the girls just stay inside and talk.

The old men in front of the country store
aren't sitting and chatting anymore.
Both storyteller and liar
set blandly inside talking by the fire.

Mister Brown debates within his mind,
Should the lawn be mowed just one last time?
Mrs. Brown standing by the door
suggests he trims the bush once more.

Distant sounds as birds flee south,
the scent of foliage dying out,

bending to season as it should
as decay settles over the neighborhood.

Common things that I once knew,
simple pleasures I looked forward to,
like leaves of summer turned to brown,
decomposing on the ground.

Contentment soon began to fade
when summer leaves gave up her shade,
like the love I thought I'd never find,
so I turned to leave it all behind.

My life a movie, black and white.
Scant of day, of ample night.
Unaware in my autumn day
God had reserved your love for me.

I whisper softly for a sign
of hope in this faded world of mine.
Then behind me one last sight I see
what Providence preserved for me.

One little bush stands off alone
beside an empty house unknown
and its bare little branches does expose
the unnoticed presence of one last rose.

The Meadow

The meadows sway in silent dance
caressed by an amorous breeze.
Fields of flowers move as one
like waves upon the sea.

Little bees court her blossoms
and taste her nectar sweet
and pollen bright as morning sun
clings to their hollow feet.

Let me take you to the meadows.
We will bask in gentle sun
and rest among the flowers
in a sea that flows as one.

On Crimson Wings

Born with wings that could not fly
into the boundless azure sky,
whose wondrous mysteries could not be found
by one whose wings were earthly bound.

The eagle was gone, she could not protest
when the egg was stolen from her nest.
It was placed beneath a barnyard hen,
was hatched and thus its life began.

Raised as a chick with a chicken mind
of its true nature it was surely blind,
fenced in by wire that did surround
this eagle who was earthly bound.

One fateful day he heard the cry
of a majestic eagle in the sky.
Something deep inside him stirred
realizing he was no common bird.

His heart was quickened by the sound.
He ran, then lifted from the ground.

His eagle nature could not ignore
he was an eagle born to soar.

Are your wings stained with barnyard mud?
Just wash them in the cleansing blood
and rise above sins fatal sting
soaring high above with crimson wings.

God endued you with the best
but Satan stole you from his nest
and put you inside a barnyard fence
to live a life of false pretense.

But from Gods voice you cannot hide
when he speaks, his voice you'll recognize
and with soaring wings you'll reach the sky
knowing you were born to fly.

Lovers Leap

Upon this cliff in Mineral Town, I stand on Lovers Leap.
I gaze on rapids far below; cold, forlorn, and deep.
They swirl and leap in the night in their angry flow.
Should I take that fatal step or should I turn and go.

But deep inside something jumps and shakes me from my trance.
What if some way, somewhere, some time, I'd have another chance.
Just then in velvet darkness a shooting star steals my sight.
I raise my collar, I turn my back, and walk into the night.

Rose

Kelly Lowery was a fighter who stayed within the ring.
No one could defeat him or stand up to his swing.
None could get him cornered or catch him in a doze,
Until his heart got cornered by a girl whose name was Rose.

When salvation came he left the ring to fight for his dear Lord,
Traveling with his companion that truly loved the Word.
Rose stood beside him through the years, through good times and the poor.
She was a blessing and a help meet and each year he loved her more.

Surely Kelly loved the flowers that each season would unfold,
The carnation and the tulip and the golden marigold,
The tantalizing tansy that taunts the senses as it grows,
But he found no flower with such beauty as his sweet and lovely Rose.

Yes, such virtue, sweet and gentle as the mornings misty dew,
That falls on springtime meadows as the flowers bloom anew.
Never hurting, never pushing, just as twilight freshly born,
Surely God had now created a Rose without a thorn.

One day God decided a bouquet he would make,
And searched the whole world over for flowers he would take.
He chose the best, the beautiful, but one stood out alone,
A wonderful and thornless Rose to now adorn his home.

It was hard for her good husband to tell his wife goodbye,
As his Rose closed her petals and gently shut her eyes.
His world collapsed, his heart did break, he thought his world would end,
But he stands with perseverance, he will see his Rose again.

Her life has been a story with so very much to tell.
She now rests until that hour she awaited for so well.
On resurrection morning she shall rise from sweet repose,
Leaving nothing here behind . . . except a grave without a Rose.

(Authors tribute to his aunt – Rose Lowery)

The Sheep

Alone, aloft, above the sea
forlorn in thought upon the pier.
His eyes behold the sun sink low
as ore' his face a salty tear

Falls gently down his weathered face,
remembering the past
as he hears a haunting distant sound
recognizing what it is at last.

He hears the bleating of the sheep
in the waves upon the sea.
The salty blood of Christ he smells
in the salty winds decree.

He lingers in the languish
recalling those he failed,
as the bleating of the waves
filter through a tattered sail.

The sky turns dark, he turns to leave,
and longing to be free,
he lies upon his bed, then dreams
of waves upon the sea.

The Portrait

My portrait proud upon the wall
crowned with gilded golden frame.
Great dreams in my eyes and smile
hung on a nail for quite a while.

What shook the house I know not at all.
Perhaps some settling of the ground.
But the nail gave way to sudden fall
and left it shattered in the hall.

The glitter in my eyes was marred
by splintered glass that wove a web
ore' my smile and left a shard
upon my portrait hurt and scarred.

People gathered and they asked,
"Why not piece it together again?"
But such a miracle would not last
to make a portrait of shattered glass.

Still I hung it on the wall,
Yet I threw the shattered shards away.
It was then behind the glass I saw
my portrait had survived the fall.

The Chosen Angel

Brilliant angels dance in scenic splendor.
In grand array they far outshine the sun.
Yet in this great multitude of beauty
My eyes transfix on only one.

This shining star is God's own chosen.
Her essence glows softly through her face.
Like tender moonlight kissing darkness,
Caressing the night sphere with her grace.

This creature garbed in royal satin,
Diamond eyes that sparkle God's own mind.
Rose petal lips as sweet as natures breezes,
A heart that is pure, sweet and kind.

Though magnificent is all of Heavens angels,
This one on earth shines brighter through the hue.
If you ask me how I know, I know that angel
For that special angel, my love, is you.

(Written for Rebecca in 1976)

*U*nstoppable

The storms of wind and time assail
And strike as flames of a burning hell
And peoples words may push and shove
But none of these can stop my love.

I'll love you when the suns' around.
I'll love you when the sun is down.
My love was destined from earth's dawn.
Somehow I'll love you when earth is gone.

So forgive me please for the way I feel,
But inside me dwells a love that's real.
So if I can't share with you a home,
Then I'll love you forever all alone.

(Written for Rebecca in 1978 or 79)

I Refuse to say Goodbye

Her hands were warm and gentle when I was born that day.
She held me to her bosom, afraid I'd get away.
As the nurse came to get me, a tear fell from her eye.
She said, "I'll see you later, I refuse to say goodbye."

She made each day a fantasy I experienced with joy
As she created new adventures playing with my toys.
I never worried about the future nor concerned with what had been.
I was taught to love each moment, the moment I was in.

Her hands were warm and gentle, preparing my first school day.
She held me to her bosom, afraid I'd get away.
When the bus came to get me a tear filled her eye.
She said, "I'll see you later, I refuse to say goodbye."

She sopped my fevered brow each time I had the flu
And kissed away my heartaches as I swiftly grew.
Soon I had grown, found a wife, and on my wedding day
My mother looked into my eyes not knowing what to say.

Her arms were warm and gentle on my wedding day
As she held me to her bosom afraid I'd get away.

With the wedding march beginning, a tear filled her eye.
She said, "I'll see you later. I refuse to say goodbye."

Two grandchildren we did give her and every single holiday
When it came time to leave her, she'd beg for us to stay.
She loved them it was plain to see, they were her pride and joy.
She showered them with love the way she raised her boy.

One day a horrid illness struck it's venom in her frame.
She crumbled like the autumn leaves, it left her hurt and maimed.
I watched my precious mother as she struggled with her pain
As she reached a withered hand toward me, whispering my name.

One day the Lord desired to make a beautiful bouquet.
He foraged plains and forests to find the best for his display.
It was then he saw a flower that surpassed all he had sown
And he knew without hesitation he'd take this flower home.

I knelt down at her bedside and wept with bitter tears.
But her loving eyes did ease me, buffering my fears.
I watched her close her weary eyes and take her final breath
As the tender blossom folded, picked by the hand of death.

My arms were warm and gentle when she died that day.
I held her to my bosom, afraid she'd get away.
When Jesus came to get her, a tear fell from my eye.
I said, "I'll see you later, I refuse to say goodbye.

It is Night

The stars are garbed in celestial light,
The moon in silence stares.
Darkness has fallen a blanket of felt,
Spiders prepare their snares.

The sky has arched a huge black dome
Which forms an eerie light.
The wind sweeps gently across the earth
And whispers, "It is night."

1969

The Return

"In the air is the future scent of snow.
Fall is gone, now I must go,"
Thus spoke the robin to Makayla;
Spoke to her so she would know.

"In winter months you will not hear me.
My heart will ache that you're not near me.
But thoughts of you my dear Makayla
Is all that I will need to cheer me.

"But the day will come, I'll spread my wings
Then on your windowsill in spring
I'll return to you, my sweet Makayla,
I'll return to you and sing."

Ocean Talk

The washing of the ocean waves,
Sunshine on the pebbled shore.
Grit and grime hugs my feet,
Meandering thoughts my mind ignores.

I look, I see, I do not think,
I feel the oceans vast expanse.
I cannot grasp the grander purpose
Of things they say are left to chance.

Came I from this salty womb,
A prokaryote from primordial soup,
Conceived by seed from celestial stone
That plunged the deep in a fiery swoop?

Did fire and water create the steam
That made my mortal being?
In briny deep does mother sleep
'Neath the vast blue world I'm seeing?

Crawled I from her nursing breast
To a new world made of land

And slowly rise toward the sky
'Till I was made to stand?

What secrets does she safely guard,
What secrets does she hide
Miles below in salty dark
Beneath the swelling tide?

But whence came she, who birthed her wave
When all was dead and night?
Did something hover over her
And say, "Let there be light?"

Did I crawl from her wet embrace
To struggle upon land
Or was I created from the dust
Created as a man?

My thoughts are shaken by a wave
That sprays its mist on me
As though she has taken notice
Of who I am, what I may be.

She looks, she sees, she does not think,
She feels my souls vast expanse.
She cannot grasp the grander purpose,
I was created and made, but not by chance.

The tide then in disappointment ebbs
To think that her son I am not
As a swelling tide of a voice inside
Assures me I was made by God.

Just Close Your Eyes

He said, "Why are you leaving?
I built us a home,
gave you all that you wanted."
She said, "You left me alone."

He cried, "I never left you.
I came home each night
and I laid right beside you."
She said, "Your eyes were closed tight.

"They were closed to my need
for someone to care
and for someone to hold me
and thoughts we could share.

"Yes, you built me a house.
You never made me a home.
Yes, you always were with me,
but I was always alone.

"When I first met you
there was a light in your eyes.
Now the flame is an ember.
Long ago the flame died.

"You closed your eyes
to my hurt and my pain.
You closed your eyes
each time I whispered your name.

"You closed your eyes .
You never saw me alone.
So just close your eyes
and you won't see me go."

The Broken Fiddle

Forgotten in the attic
lay a fiddle tired and worn.
Its keys fell off and strings unwound.
Its bow was frayed and torn.

Once it filled the house with music
in the fiddlers joyous clutch.
Now completely disassembled
it lay silent in the dust.

A knock upon the door
revealed an old man in the snow.
Frozen snowflakes in his bushy brow,
he had no where to go.

The snow was falling hard and fast.
Night would be here soon.
So he was granted just one night
of sleep in the attic room.

The next morning dawned with great surprise.
They woke to sweet serenade
of majestic sounds of music
from the attic being made.

Astonished they asked how he could put
the fiddle together again.
He smiled before he replied,
"I made this violin."

The music swelled the rafters
and stirred up ancient dust
with notes of adulation
from the floorboards to the truss'.

So if your life is in pieces
invite the Maker in
and he'll turn your broken fiddle
into a beautiful violin.

When my Season Comes

The forest green turns to brown,
lifeless leaves fall to the ground.
But this picture of death is not the end.
The forest green shall live again.

A planted seed dies in the earth
and from this death springs forth a birth.
From fruit that died, its seed was covered,
in spring a brand new fruit discovered.

So take this body and lay it down.
Bury it deep within the ground.
When spring to me my God shall send,
I shall rise and live again.

Leaves That Were Green

The leaves turn brown,

        Fluttering slowly down,

                Resting silently on frozen ground.

In the dark of space

        The sun turns its face,

                Winter comes to take its place.

My warm heart turns cold

        As I grow old,

                Soon my weary arms shall fold.

The leaves turn brown,

        Fluttering down,

                Resting above me on frozen ground.

Dad or Fool

Any fool can sire a child, 'tis true and yet so sad,
But it takes a *special* kind of man for a child to call a dad.
He doesn't *tell* you how to live and hope you make it through it.
A father strives to live the life and lets you *watch* him do it.

The greatest gift a child is ever given from its father
is given when he shows the child how much he loves their mother
and shows by deed and not by word what really makes a man,
so what is seen, not what is heard, is what they understand.

Great degrees a child receives from any school or college
cannot compare to what is gleaned from his fathers knowledge.
Lessons learned cannot be framed on a wall for all to see.
It is carried with him in the heart wherever he may be.

It's not the seed that you passed on that makes a man a dad.
It's being an example and giving all the love you had.
Any fool can sire a child, 'tis sad and yet so true,
When he is grown it will be known if you were dad or fool.

The Hero

"We interrupt this program," I heard the announcer say,
"to bring this special announcement, someone special arrived today."
Reporters were all around him, lights were flashing, cameras rolled.
They said this fireman was a hero who saved a five year old.

We often hear of many heroes in the evening news
and listen to the accolades of the newsworthy acts they do.
But there's another type of hero that we never hear about
whose weekly acts of sacrifice are never pointed out.

She never braved a fire just to save a five year old,
but she braved a world set on fire saving lives the Devil stole.
Little hearts and little souls, scarred by deeds so cruel,
she touched with her healing message in her Sunday School.

The abused, the hurting and those others forgot
she reached with Christs' love and the message that he taught.
With tender hearts they listened to every word she had to say
and when they left they did not forget, the truth, the life, the way.

Sometimes we forgot her, to show how much we cared.
She never appeared on TV for all the love she shared.
She never had a following, she never had a fan,
but she had a lot of children who called her Mommy Jan.

She never received a medal, she was never on the news
for all the lives she led to Jesus, for all the ones that she prayed through.
But when the saints are finally taken and the final roll is called,
she will enter Heavens portals, with his glory to behold.

"We interrupt this program," she will hear the announcer say,
"to bring this special announcement, someone special arrived today.
My dear, the crowds that run to meet you, each one in your crown a jewel.
These are the children you brought with you — this is your Sunday School."

(Authors tribute to his mother-in-law ~ Janet Settle)

Meditation

Meditation, Meditation
Mantra, mantra, concentration.
Just a mental stimulation
of the mind's misinformation.
Such a discombobulation
of a brain put out of gear.
The mind would better fare
in just a little time of prayer,
then the mind could clearly see
a mighty God that is not me.

Both Day and Night

I would have no reservation for proper meditation,
But meditation for meditation's sake does not illumination make.
Yet for a certain contemplation on the name and on the Word
I would have no hesitation and the same is much preferred.

The Stolen Rose

In the sweet misery of summer I first beheld your face,
like a rose in a crowded garden, ensnared in a briary place.
I strained to watch you longer, I stood transfixed, transposed,
but the crowd your image swept away just like a stolen rose.

Summer passed, winter came, summer bloomed again.
In a small unguarded garden I watched as you walked in.
Hair that flowed, light blue eyes, lips of fair rose red,
I wished to say "I love you," but stammered to you instead.

Of all the flowers in the terrace I could have picked that day,
the only one I wanted was the one that got away.
How they swiftly took you from me, Heaven only knows.
They took you from my little garden, just like a stolen rose.

Your family took you home with them, I went to mine.
But that night I dreamed of the day our lives would intertwine.
I was too young to understand, you were too young to bloom.
You needed time for growing, I needed growing too.

Then just a few weeks later sitting by the lake,
together sharing moments as memories we made.
That week went fast, youth camp was gone, it was time to go.
Your family came to take you home, just like a stolen rose.

You went to your home and family, I went to mine.
But again I dreamed of the day our lives would intertwine,
when we would be one, forever one, and you would never go,
leaving me mourning for my little stolen rose.

On a tree in a shaded park we etched our names in love,
savoring the flowers, the meadows green, and the sky above.
One day I got the courage to hold your soft sweet hand.
It seemed the tide was more than I, the mortal heart, could stand

By the fountain, on my knee, the day had now arrived.
I gave to you a flower with a diamond ring inside.
I knew you were the one with whom I'd spend my life
I gave you the flower asking, "Will you be my wife?"

We traveled the whole world over, working for the King.
Through good times and the rough, together we did cling.
On a missionary trip one day I was called to go.
Customs pushed you from me just like a stolen rose.

Through the years I watched you blossom to who you are today
and I cherish every moment that we shared along the way.
We are much older now and older we shall grow,
but stronger is the love we shared as kids so long ago.

One day perhaps an angel will take one of us in death
leaving us separated only by our mortal breath.
For you no more poetry will I be able to compose
when you are taken from me just like a stolen rose.

But the one left behind should not dwell in grief.
We will meet again in Heaven, our separation shall be brief.
One day together we shall be and when that chapter closes,
we'll spend eternity in a place where there are no stolen roses.

Sand

They burned our temple to the ground,
left us shrouded
in the dust of its ashes,
ashes mixed with blood,
blurring our vision
as we stumbled over steaming stone and broken arrows.
Laughter rising from a distant cloud
fleeing with its bounty.
Must we be beaten with mercy
and solaced by judgment?
By whose hand are we shielded or smitten?
The cries of our little ones fading in the crashing silence,
their dying whimpers now drowned out
by the wailing of mothers
in the aftermath of war.
They had unmercifully stolen the golden seat of our God,
and now they have taken his empty room
leaving us with memories of promises
in the ashes mixed with the coagulated blood of the stricken.
Shall they too steal our empty hearts and empty hands
and scatter us abroad the face of the earth
meandering and wandering aimlessly without measure?

Only to be brought together again to watch our holy hill
desecrated by those who call on Diana by another name,
confusing us, amusing us, confounding our children
to the point we no longer know
if it is Diana camouflaged by gender
or our God by some other name.
And we cry.
The blast of the wind scars our flesh with sand.
Our calloused knees rock back and forth on the pavement before our promise.
And we cry.
Ancient words from ancient script we utter from without within.
Hear our prayer, our ancient prayer,
our determined, ragged, surviving prayer.
And we cry.
Where is our King, where is his stallion,
his sword and his shield and his oil and wine?
He shall return.
And we shall see him.
Open our eyes that we may know him.
When he comes.
When he comes.
When he comes.
And we cry.

In the Palm

In the beginning was the end,
if the beginning by any other name is just as sweet.
When what is, was what was
in just another form
unseparated by time.
All was but a thought in the eternal mind
when he spoke.
Yehiy, Vayehiy.
A naked singularity,
an immensely primordial word
pregnant with the universe.
Like a histrionic exploding sun
All burst forth from the fetal statement
in a molten explosion of beingness,
of energy, of fire,
of light, and of sound.
Forms shot through nothing
making something through which to travel.
Burning, blazing, bouncing, cooling,
creating destination, pure form concentration.
Seething, searing, sighing.

Obeying the echoes of the ancient word.
While peering from behind a wall of nothingness
the planner paused to see
a trillion brilliant galaxies unfolding like a rose.
To plant a seed in the center was impossible to do,
For that which has no outside has no center it can choose.
An arm unfolded from the Milky Way
and on the edge its hand outstretched
and in its palm it held the seed of which
would one day become my home.
In the palm of the hand of this galaxy
which dwelt in the palm of another
unfolded all of history,
it's triumphs, love, and tragedy
Moses, Buddha, Christ, and Gandhi
Plato, Shakespeare, Mozart and Monet
Emerson, Kant, Thoreau and Spinoza
Galileo, Newton, Einstein and Hawking
The electric Kool-Aid acid test
Dylan, Leary, love, and flowers
Al-Qa'ida, and the twin towers
War, death, conquest, and blood.
Armageddon, Armageddon.
Four horsemen on the prowl.
The nations crying for a savior,
one who speaks great words.
Great words of peace, just take his name,

his number or his name.
Babylon the great he courts.
The world spins 'round, faster, faster
I, me , mine toward disaster.
Greed, death, selfish endeavors.
People attempting to outdo each other.
Like the dinosaurs man has run his course.
The trumpet sounds.
All rebounds.
All rebounds.
Returning from whence it came.
The Yehiy and Vayehiy
The first and the last,
the beginning and the end.
All rebounds.
And what was, becomes what is.
In the end is the beginning,
if the end by any other name is just as sweet.

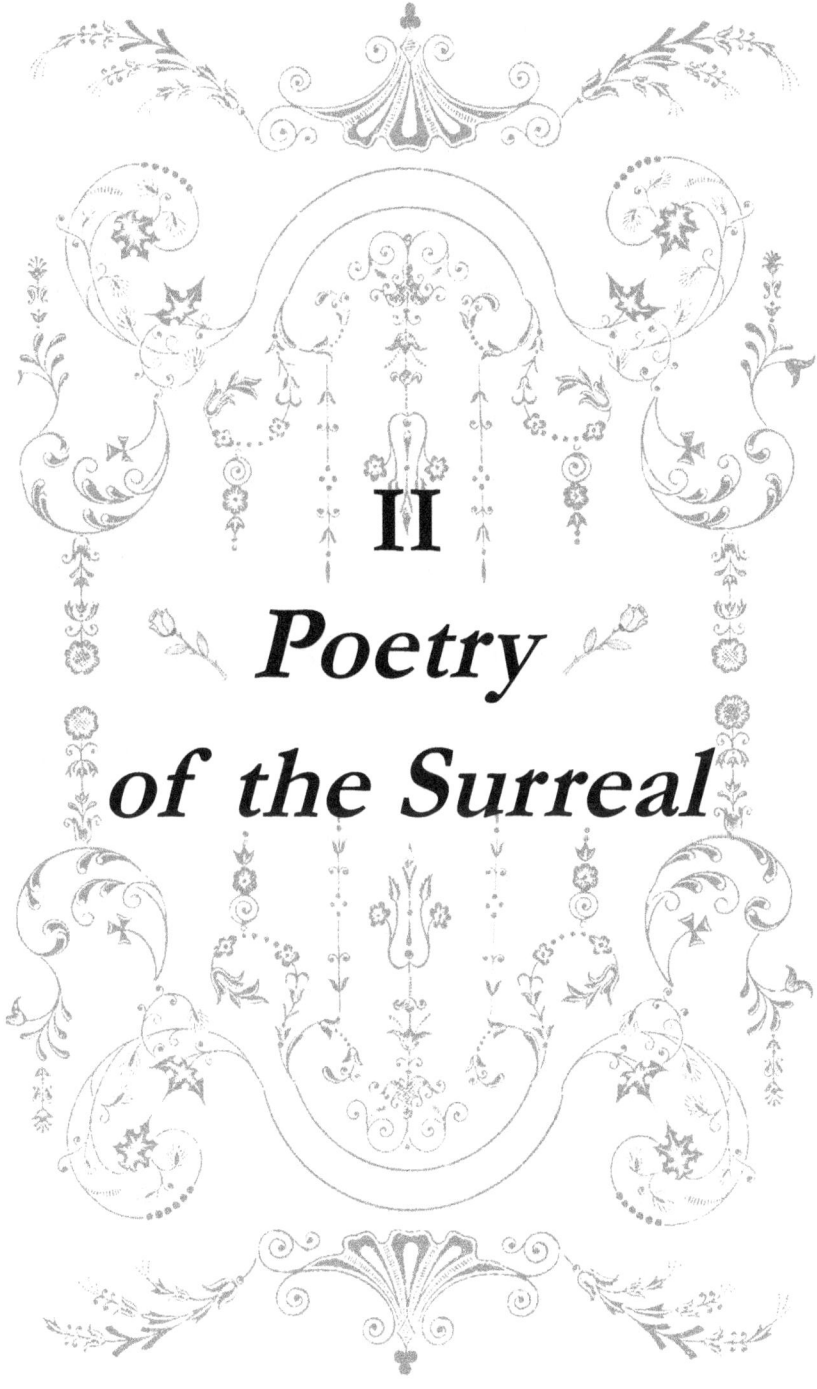

II
Poetry of the Surreal

The Ghost of Orange

She was sitting at her wooden table, eating from her wooden ladle
When in the corner of her eye she saw, an image cast upon her wall.
She commenced to leap upon her feet, but her legs were frozen to her seat
Before a bowl of curdled porridge,
From the presence of the ghost of Orange.

She forced her eyes toward the wall, where she thought she saw the image fall.
The wall was barren, cold, and still, haunting gray from floor to ceil'.
What she could not see she now could hear, and falling on her fearful ear
The creaking of the cabin door-hinge
From the presence of the ghost of Orange.

Fireplace flames in calm retention, the image was not their invention.
If it came not from their amber stall, what formed the specter on the wall?
Prince William surely could not have known, the plot her former spouse had sown
From the seed she planted in his head
Before the royal blood was shed.

The image flashed, the door did creak, she felt her limbs becoming weak.
She felt his presence in the room, his musty spirit from the tomb.
She threw her bowl at the fire, which sent the flames reaching higher,

But flames could not chase nor singe
The laughter of the ghost of Orange.

Choked with fear she stood up straight, fled through the door then through the gate.
Running fast, running faster, she could not outrun his laughter.
As she ran she held her ears, but nothing could dispel her fear.
Naught could slow the exortinge
Or the laughter of the ghost of Orange.

Upon the hills of lilting silver, cast on lazy curls of chilver,
Sleepy sheep looked up to see, this woman in a frantic flee.
Perhaps her person could not be seen, by hiding in the dark ravine,
Beside the lofty hills of Blorange,
Hiding from the ghost of Orange.

"Arise, arise," the phantom cried, "there is no place where you can hide.
My spirits' restless from the strife of those who strove to take my life."
"Away away," she did reply, "you're just a figment of my mind!"
But she knew a sworn avenge
Burned within ghost of Orange.

Around the moon an eerie circle, a darkened shade of scarlet purple.
Midnight mist dropped like blood, turning soil into mud.
The urge to run again was tempting, but she had no strength, her soul was empty.
Her dire deed did not anticipate
One day her deed would seal her fate.

"What horror did the pit unleash, whence came this dark nocturnal beast
What fear and rage have fallen off, the person of this raging wolf
And quickly settled in my being, to paralyze the world I'm seeing,
And brings my soul into submission
To this malicious apparition?"

Her fear of death became his power, what she gave him made her cower
In her sulking trembling frame, from his ominous ocherous flame.
Then suddenly upon her feet, trembling legs found strength to leap
And ran 'til she could feel no more.
Ran 'til she was numb and sore.

Up ahead a cliff so steep, the ravine below was dark and deep.
Her frantic run began to slow, stopped at the edge, then peered below.
The ghostly fiend was gaining fast, she took the step, peace at last.
Falling she heard a deafening sound.
Her heart exploded 'fore hitting the ground.

Rousing from her sleep of death, she gasped out for a single breath.
Fire around her raged in heat, a cocoon of flames from head to feet.
"You'll not escape my words of terror, you're here," he cried, "with me forever
Where naught can flee nor obstringe
The laughter of the ghost of Orange!"

This poem about the assassinated Prince of Orange (fourteenth century) contains five words (including "orange") which are said to rhyme with no other words in the English lannguage. Does this poem succeed in rhyming them?

The Crimson Wolf

In the stillness, in the silence, a presence gliding through the night,
Swiftly leaping through the shadows completely out of sight.
Diana casts her moonlight on the harlot sleeping sound,
Completely unsuspecting, lying on the open ground.

Out of the dark, through glaring teeth, breaks forth a piercing howl.
The creature wakes the woman whose hot anger is aroused.
Into the the night he leaps again leaving behind the daughter
For other wolves as he proceeds on the trail to find the mother.

Three moons shall pass for healing of the creatures wounded head
Then he shall return to see indeed if the daughter is truly dead.
To the other wolves it will be revealed they had a common cause
With the wounded, unrelenting, blood covered crimson wolf.

The Jester

He was tired, he was tattered, he was ravaged with disease.
He was begging on the corner; he was begging for relief.
People chattered, people jostled as they bobbled to and fro,
in a hurry, in a hurry, with no special place to go.

He felt someone was watching, watching him too close.
That was when he saw the jester on the corner in repose.
He was leaning on a street lamp, grinning, smiling with a glare,
laughing at the beggar and the clothes that he did wear.

Ashamed the beggar closed his eyes, but opened them again
to find the jester in his face with a taunting grin.
"Today I have an offer, one you can't refuse,"
Thus spake the smiling jester, "I have a gift for you."

"You can use it, don't refuse it, it will turn your rags to gold.
It will make you feel much warmer, instead of oh so cold."
He then held forth a shining fruit, glaring with a grin,
"Take it, it will make you forget the pain you're in.

"This is yours, you deserve it, I prepared it just for you
with magic and with mystery; won't you take the tour?"
A voice then danced in rhythm above the chatter of the crowd
Words of a soapbox orator that slowly grew more loud.

The oration like an arrow pierced the beggars heart of stone,
"Though you have not many riches, your soul is all you own.
Store in your heart the greatest gifts, life's greatest treasures.
Don't sell your heart, don't sell your soul for temporary pleasures."

"Listen, listen, you must listen," the jester did now shout,
frowning in his new attempt to drown the speaker out.
"Take a bite, it will change you, you never will be old
and all your soiled garments will turn to woven gold."

The beggar looked into the window, his reflection shook it's head,
but he heeded not the warning, he ate the fruit instead.
He was suddenly in the window. His reflection on the walk,
as he gazed on in horror, in his terror and his shock.

A golden gilded jester robed gayly now was he,
but trapped in this reflection, never to be free.
Watching his reality begging for some food,
caught in his illusion, a reflection of a fool.

The beggar on the sidewalk suddenly fell dead,
but the jester in the window lived on and on instead.
His soul and heart he traded for things that would not last
and all he left behind was a reflection in the glass.

The Woman of my Dreams

The mist of dawn does well diffuse
the nebulous image with lassitude.
A languorous dream whose secret fate
is to reveal itself and scintillate.
The image now becomes much clearer
as the image now comes much nearer.
Her misty air I almost taste
as mist divides to show her face.
The vision I behold it seems
reveals the woman of my dreams.
Is she real, what is this I see,
a vision of one that was meant for me?
Why do I see her? From whence she came?
Do I hallucinate or do I dream?
Do I create the image from the fog
or is this a vision sent from God?
The evanescent image fades
with the ephemeral elation it creates.
And now there is nothing there
except her imprint in the air.
I see her lips cherry red,
a golden halo 'round her head,
pure blue eyes that melt my heart
and revives an ember to a fire.

Where did she go, I cannot see,
this lovely vision that flees from me.
I close my eyes, open them again
and find myself upon this bed
of sickness with a fevered brow.
"I think that he can hear us now,"
she said as she held my hand.
I looked at her, and I looked again.
Through hazy eyes I saw my wife
the angelic lover of my life.
The mist of dawn does well diffuse
the nebulous image with lassitude.
A languorous dream whose secret fate
is to reveal itself and scintillate.
The image now becomes much clearer
as the image now comes much nearer.
I see her lips cherry red,
a golden halo 'round her head,
pure blue eyes that melt my heart
and revives an ember to a fire.
Whence she came, I now can see
the woman that God gave to me.
I close my eyes, my vision grows dim.
I know I shall see my love again
on some far and distant shore
where her image will fade no more.
No longer an image she will always be
the woman of my dreams.

III
Little Songs of Love

Beckyville

Walk with me,

Talk with me,

And you'll never be alone.

Come with me to Beckyville

And you shall find a home.

In Beckyville there is no sorrow.

The glory of the Lord fills her home.

There's no yesterday, only tomorrow

And Becky will never be alone.

Run with me

Through the park.

Swing upon the swings.

We'll swing so high, we'll touch the sky,

We'll do so many things.

Come with me to the fountain

And look so deep within my eyes.

Together we'll climb every mountain

And Becky will never be alone.

(Song the author wrote for Rebecca in 1976)

My Little Angel Girl

High above the city lights,
The Olentangy River.
Dining in an atmosphere
Of the twelfth of never.
I look so deep within your eyes
As I say, "Be my girl."
And now, yes now
You're my little Angel Girl.

*(Song written for Rebecca in 1976
after the author asked her to 'go steady' with him)*

IV
Collected Poetry

The Elder's Song

There was a man; he was a man of the Word,
Who traveled abroad doing God's work.
This one was quite a man you see,
He threw out the lifeline that rescued me.

He came to our church and began to sing.
His resounding voice made the rafters ring.
His song was so powerful and full of might,
I ran to the altar, where God gave me sight.

Of the many souls that I would win,
He inspired me to rescue them from sin.
I was only seven when this man touched my heart.
Our destiny then moved us so far apart.

Years went by and I saw him no more,
Until one day he stepped through the door.
The anointing fell, I heard his song and said,
I know this voice, I know this man.

Yes, this was that man God sent that day
when I was a child to show me the way.
Though sickness and pain he often was in,
This great man of valor still reached those in sin.

A truer prophet I could not find.
His words still echo in my mind.
"Sister, till Jesus comes don't give up the fight.
Go, go, go with all your might!"

He taught me to sing and I'll pass it on
for another to sing one day when I'm gone.
Then the song will live forever, you see,
The song from the heart of God's man-
      Elder Alfred Tyree!

By Rebecca Ward
(Author's wife)
1999

Time

Time, time, watch it fly.
Faster, faster, speeding by.
I don't know why it keeps on going
without pausing or even slowing.

Spin, spin, watch it spin.
The world goes 'round that we live in.
As I age I begin to fear
the end of life is drawing near.

Older, older, I can't erase
the wrinkles time leaves on my face.
So since I cannot slow time down
I'll enjoy my time while I'm still around.

By Brandon Ward
(Author's son)
2005

Woolyburger Hill

We held hands and stood silently still
in the cemetery on top of Woolyburger Hill.

Shadows arched their wicked backs to claim your stature
but your melancholy beauty was too violent to capture.
Our passion was a rhapsodic fruit hanging from the tree
but the fruit did die and transformed a noose around me.

The virgin sky parted and soft raindrops fell,
releasing heavy screaming, whispers from hell.
The irony was almost too much to withstand
that Heaven could release chaos on command.

Bleak was the moist ground that shut up their bones,
distraught to discover these were our tombstones.
Your emeralds were difficult treasures to fill
as we laid here slumberless on Woolyburger Hill.

By Makayla Ward

(Author's daughter)

2010

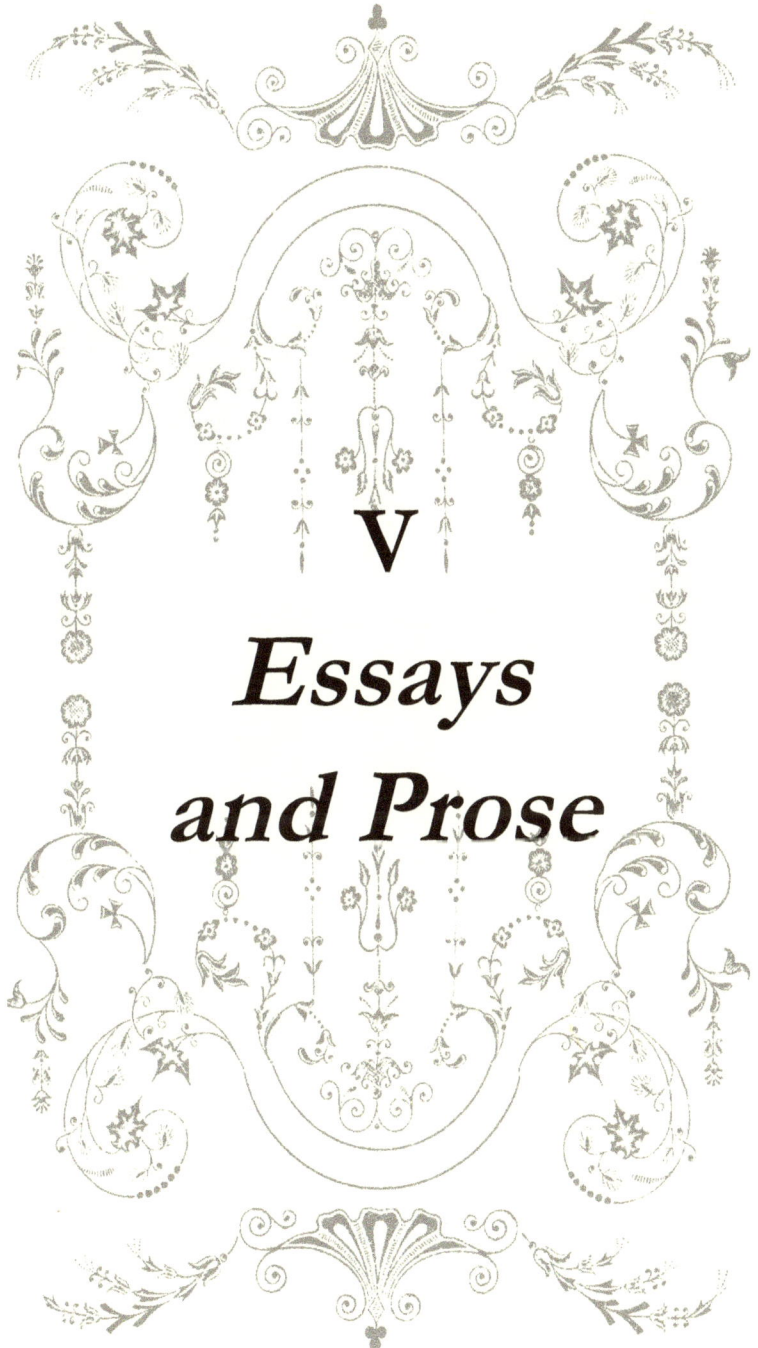

V

Essays and Prose

The Old Guitar

The day they lowered my father into his grave was the day I realized that nothing in this world is permanent. I had just lost my mother a year before and I now felt like an abandoned orphan without hope of ever finding the old homestead again.

My father was a jovial person. He was entertaining, sometimes wise, and sometimes unpredictable. He had a great love for music and we oftentimes would sit out on the old front porch and pick our guitars to the accompaniment of a nearby field of crickets that suddenly came alive at dusk. The lonely howl of a dog on the other side of the village joined our serenade. The sweet smell of decaying wood drifted from the hillside from behind the old homestead and in the crisp evening air I felt a feeling of "forever."

Dad had an old Gibson guitar he had purchased from someone for thirty five dollars. He ended up buying a more expensive one and I ended up with the old Gibson. As the years hurried by like the autumn leaves that danced through our village street, I watched my father age. By the time I left home Dad had accumulated a nice collection of musical instruments. I took the old Gibson with me. He knew I had it.

Some years later I found out that the old Gibson had increased in value. One day as he visited with me I shared with him the great increase in value the guitar had. He looked at me with a wry grin and said, "I never did give you that guitar, did I? You just up and claimed it." Although I thought I remembered that at one point he had given it to me, I had never really given it much thought. With his wry humor he had let me know it was just borrowed. At his remark we both laughed.

When my mother was diagnosed with cancer, my father's world collapsed. Things that never bothered him before became mountains of agitation. One day he borrowed the guitar. He never brought it back. Sometime later when I was sorting through stacks of memorabilia in their back room, the old Gibson caught the corner of my eye. I noticed he had tried to varnish it and I panicked. I knew his good intentions were going to ruin the value of this ancient musical piece. Since the old Gibson and I had been pals for so many years I thought nothing of taking it back home with me. When I related this to Dad a few days later, he exploded. When I forgot to bring it with me the next time I visited him, it was "hail Columbia!" He told me there was going to be trouble if he didn't receive it back. I looked into those hurting angry eyes and realized it wasn't really me he was disturbed with, it was my mothers cancer.

I took the guitar to my sister's house one morning, knowing he was visiting that day, and left it with a note that said, "To Dad with love." When he saw it he told me to go ahead and keep the guitar. I said, "No, that's O.K. Dad, I can borrow it sometimes." I shall never forget the sight of my aging father as he trotted away from that house in shallow victory. He had won the guitar but he had not defeated Mom's cancer. He was walking in a stream that flowed with both sweet and bitter waters. The decoy for his anger was gone and the arrow of pain found its target. Many changes took place in him the months ahead. They were all good changes. Changes took place in me as well.

The day they were about to lower my father into his grave I threw myself across the cold, hard casket and wept bitter tears. I felt a grand loss of something that I thought was "forever." There would be no more fishing trips with him on warm summer days. There would be no more sleigh rides with him on the white crusted slopes in our little village.

But then I realized . . . he wasn't really mine. He was God's. I just borrowed him.

Like the old Gibson my memories of him increase in value each and every fleeting day. But these too are just borrowed. Wherever such things ultimately go to, wherever my Dad has gone, I too shall go. When I arrive perhaps we will share our music together again serenaded by angels rather than by crickets. Perhaps there will be a fishing hole there and crisp spring evenings that sharpen our senses. Perhaps I'll find that old homestead I have so longed for. Something tells me that when I do, this time I will find "forever."

Grandma

I awoke to the smell of bacon frying in the pan as my closed eyelids were gently assaulted by the morning sunlight. A shiver of excited contentment ran though me as I remembered I had stayed at Grandma's house last night.

Opening my hesitant eyes I could see the kitchen through the doorway of my little bedroom. Standing in front of the kitchen stove was the familiar figure of my grandmother. Her small frame hovered over the pan as well withered arthritic hands shook the skillet and flipped the bacon over. The morning sunlight that awoke me now glistened and danced in the silver strands of her hair. Her faded dress revealed patterns of fading flowers I had not noticed last night. She seemed like a precious relic of a long forgotten world, a quaint reminder of a kinder time, a coelacanth in an age of frenzied technology.

I shall never forget those cheery mornings with Grandma. Her humble little home and her simple possessions seemed like glistening treasures to a little boy away from home. Even though she is long gone I often go back to Grandma's house. I just close my eyes as my memory is gently assaulted by morning sunlight until once again I see her standing once more in that doorway.

The Kiss I Never Gave Her

The twigs broke softly beneath our feet as we walked through the woods adjoining the little park. The sunlight played hide and seek through the leaves of the trees that were fluttering in the gentle summer breeze. The scent of wood and greenery was invigorating. The world was a very, very bright place this day. We had just swung together on the swings. I had pushed her as high as I could and I saw her glance briefly at me and I understood I had pushed the limit. She was sixteen years old and the most beautiful creature I had ever beheld. To me she was an angel. The little scenic path we were walking took us into a wooded area that was almost Edenic in nature. We were not to venture too far away from her mother's watchful eyes but it did grant us some measure of privacy. Looking back now I see that we were just kids. Two kids madly in love . . . drunk on love . . totally immersed in each other. When we looked into each others eyes the rest of the world dissipated from existence and there was only "us." One glance of her pure blue eyes melted me into a pool of bliss. We were walking a small incline now and I took her hand to assist her. The moment I touched her, the gentle warmth of her hand made my heart leap out of sync. She leaned up against a tree for a moment of rest, her blue eyes gazed toward the tree tops softly in search of the birds which were serenading this moment. She looked at me and instinctively I drew closer to her. I was so close I felt her sweet breath softly reaching out to mine. This was a magical moment. I was about to kiss her for the very first time. I had never felt so much love in my life. When first we met she appeared to me to be an angel. I would later dub her as "my little angel girl." As we gazed into each others eyes I came closer. So desperately I wanted to kiss her but I was so afraid. For minutes that seemed like eternity we lingered in that experience. We almost kissed. Almost. Our lips never met that day.

As the years passed by I often reminisced on why the magical kiss never took place that day. The moment was perfect . . . it was magical. Perhaps it was due to the fact that right after my born again Christian experience that I refused to entertain any thoughts that I deemed "carnal" in any way. Perhaps it was due to the fact that we had known each other for only a few months. Perhaps I was just plain afraid.

The following year we went back to "our" tree and we carved our names into it. Around our names we carved a valentine heart and the testament to our love is still inscribed in that tree to this very day. Occasionally we visit that park and we walk into the woods and visit our tree again. The magic is always there waiting on us. We are both much older now. We are no longer kids. The tree has also grown and aged. But the love we etched into its side is just as visible today as it was those many years ago. It is still there because we took the time to cut it deep into the side of the tree. We cut it deep enough that the winter winds and the summer storms would not be able to wear it away. We cut it deep enough that the sands of time could not diminish it's message. Yes, we occasionally go back to our tree, but sometimes years pass before we visit it. Although we do not see it during those spans of time, we know the love we carved so deeply into it's bark so very many years ago is still there.

The other morning I was in a hurry to get to an appointment. I rushed toward the door and then stopped. Something that had been carved in our hearts many, many years ago was calling me. The sands of time had not weakened it's voice. We had etched it deep enough to last. I turned around, walked toward the bedroom and cracked open our door. She was still sleeping. I briefly recalled that magical moment many years ago when I had longed to kiss her. I quietly walked over to her, bent over, and placed a gentle kiss upon her lips. For a brief moment I felt the magic. But my appointment was calling me, reminding me I had miles to go before I sleep. I turned to go and something stopped me once again. The woods were lovelier. Still dressed in my suit, I tenderly pulled back the covers and, without waking her, laid down beside her, holding her in my arms. The magic was more important than my appointment.

The tree is still in those woods. The tribute of love carved into her side will always be there. But occasionally I need to go back to the tree . . . back to our tribute . . . to recall how long it took me to finally allow our lips to meet and to savor and cherish and celebrate every moment that we are still together. We often revisit the magic. We often share again the memories. And every once in awhile we recall that day in the park and we remember how sweet was the kiss I never gave her .

Sign of a Miracle

I had seen miracles before. You never really grow used to them. They astound you each and every time. I suppose that is good; it keeps us appreciative of divine intervention in a world that is slowing unwinding in a state of entropy.

Sometimes miracles happen. Sometimes they don't. I wasn't really sure at all what was going to take place in this particular case. Most of the family was really frightened. This was someone very special to us and special people are far and few in between. She was my mother-in law. I loved her very much and couldn't bear the thought of ever losing her.

My natural mother had passed away some years before. It was a confusing circumstance. She had a fast growing cancer and the doctors had insisted on intensive chemotherapy. I insisted on intensive prayer. I felt great joy when finally the oncologist told us Mom was cancer free. He was very surprised at such a miraculous comeback. I knew it was the work of the Lord. The family began making plans on how we were going to spend the days ahead and places we would take Mother. Then suddenly she grew weak. Within twenty four hours she was gone. Although the cancer had been defeated, the cancer, and the chemo, had created irreparable damage to her internal organs. The results were unexpected . . . at least for me. After she took her last and final breath I threw myself across her and cried out asking God why would he heal her only to turn right around and allow her to die. I will never forget what God spoke to me in that moment. He said, "I wanted you to know that *cancer* didn't take her—*I* took her. I took her home." In that profound moment I realized that all was well.

There comes a time when every single one of us must hear the tolling of the bells. But this just didn't seem the right time for Janet, my mother-in-law . . . not during the time that my sister-in-law was going through the worst trial of her life. It was my deepest fear that Debbie's life hung on Jan's survival. In addition my children were still mourning the loss of my parents. We all were hoping for some kind of miracle. I'm just not sure that the family was prepared for the miracle they were about to receive.

Although the hospital room was filled with family, it suddenly became quiet when the doctor entered the room. Jan had been sick for awhile and was growing progressively worse. We had been waiting for quite awhile for the results of the biopsy and this was the moment of truth. The doctor paused, opened his folder, causally looked up at us and said, "Mrs. Settle, You have cancer."

The room went numb.

No one uttered a sound.

"Doctor," I asked, "How long does she have to live?"

I will never forget his chilling words as long as I live. "Six months. Or maybe a year."

Jan was admitted to the hospital prior to surgery because of the severity of her symptoms. She had lost a very large amount of blood due to the cancer. We were told the cancer was going into the fourth stage. The doctor said her lungs were also very weak and that she would most probably need a tracheotomy, surviving on a respirator for the remainder of her life—that is if she survived surgery. The situation seemed quite bleak.

I had been doing an in depth study on the Holy Anointing Oil of Exodus chapter 30. This oil was said to be so spiritually powerful that anything it touched became Kodesh. It was forbidden to be used on an outsider or duplicated for use by common persons. Today it is permissible to be used on born again Christians only and Janet was certainly born again. She was a woman who had completely sold out to God. Of course I was aware that there was nothing "magical" about the oil. I knew that oil didn't heal—God heals! But I also knew that many times Christ would use things as a point of contact. Since I had been sharing my studies with my mother-in-law, I knew it would be a great point of contact and a great faith builder. We began to go before the Lord in prayer before returning to the hospital. We knew that this cancer needed to be assaulted by earnest prayer.

When we entered her room there was a spirit of gloom that permeated the place. A dark cloud of despair hung over her bed. Her face was pale and lifeless. There was no hope in her eyes. After briefly visiting with her we announced that we were going to anoint her with the Holy Anointing Oil and pray for her. As we anointed and laid hands upon her something suddenly took place! The previously darkened room lit up. Jan's whole face began to light up and tears streamed from her eyes. Suddenly she cried out, "I felt something leave my body! I felt something leave my body!" The entire atmosphere was charged! Something awesome had just occurred!

The doctors were persistent they proceed with the surgery. When the day of surgery arrived we briefly spoke our last words with with her and then went downstairs to the waiting room which quickly filled with concerned family and friends. Furrowed brows, pacing feet, and monotone voices were witness to the despair and agony gnawing inside of them. Hours slowly crept by. I spent much of the time in the hospital chapel in prayer, coming back from time to time to see if any word had been received by the family. As the day crawled onward the family became increasingly fearful and agitated.

I remember the frightened look on one persons face. "We haven't heard anything yet," she said. "I think it's worse than they thought. They will probably just close her up and say there is nothing more they can do for her." I consoled her to the best of my feeble abilities and then returned to the chapel. There was something very reassuring about the chapel. There were no anxious faces, no pacing bodies, no one breaking out in cold sweats. There was no unbelief to deal with. It was a quiet place were I could listen as well as talk to the Lord. I wanted some great reassurance, some vision, some supernatural sign. Certainly I had experienced such things before. When I was three years old I heard the call to the ministry. It was many years before I really heeded the call, but I had heard it. After I had grown older and began to really live for the Lord I heard the audible voice of God. I heard a wind that began to slowly blow through my room. In that wind I heard a voice whisper, "Curtis." I raised from my bed to see who had called my name. The room was empty. The wind continued and again I heard, "Curtis." Still there was no explanation from whence the voice had come. And then a third time I heard, "Curtis . . . I have called thee." Then I knew.

Certainly God could do this again. Certainly I could have some great visitation from the Lord or some supernatural appearance of an angel . . . some sign of reassurance to take back to the grieving family. Or perhaps it was there all along. Perhaps I was looking for some spectacular spiritual phenomenon when some small sign was in front of our faces the entire time.

Had I, had *we*, been a bit more observant maybe we would not have missed the little hint of what was about to occur. Jan's nurse had been in and out of her room on several occasions and none of us had ever noticed. None of us had ever slowed down long enough to observe such a simple thing as the nurses name tag. Who does that anyway? Who reads name tags?

Some sign would have been so reassuring to us all. But as I prayed I heard no great winds and saw no mighty visions . . . I heard only a wee small voice assuring me that God still answers prayer.

Each time I returned to the waiting room the level of anxiety had risen and expectations seemed to increasingly darken. Would they discover it was too late for surgery, chemotherapy and radiation? Would they tell us the end was nearer then the original six months to a year they had grimly predicted ?

Then the hour so laboriously awaited for finally arrived.

The tall, slim doctor walked cautiously into the waiting room with a very puzzled look on his face. Immediately several family members leaped from their seats, surrounding the doctor with questions about the results of the surgery. The doctor quietly dropped his head as he looked silently into the folder he held in his hands. His long fingers nervously played with the corner of the folder and then he looked up and said, "I need to speak with the family in the counseling room." One of Jan's sisters broke into a wail, tears streaming down her face, "The only time they take you back into that room is when they have bad news to break to the family."

As we crowded into the stuffy little room some of the family was crying, others were visibly nervous, and some just went blank. The doctor leaned up against the wall, lifted the folder, and dropped his head as he looked briefly at the folder again. Yes, doctors usually take family into the back room to give them bad news, but this doctor didn't take the family back to share bad news with them . . . he took them back because he had news that he couldn't explain! "Now our records reveal that indeed this was cancer," he explained, "I have the results of the biopsy which was previously shared with you and it came back positive for cancer. She was entering the fourth stage of cancer. But . . ." he cautiously continued, "We don't understand it, but when we preformed the surgery, there was absolutely no cancer in her body."

NO CANCER!!!

The room ecstatically brightened up!

NO CANCER!!!

No tracheotomy! No respirator!

It was time to weep . . . not as the family had been weeping, but it was the season to weep for joy. There was no scientific explanation, there was no natural answer for the phenomenon, there was but one explanation and one alone—it was indeed a miracle!

As I pen these words it has been over five years ago since this series of events came to pass. Every six months my mother-in-law went to the doctor to be screened for cancer. I think they thought for sure it would have to be hiding somewhere in some remote cells somewhere in her system. They never found them. They were not there. She saw the doctor for the last time three months ago. He told her she didn't have to return for future check ups. She was declared cancer free.

She never received a cancer treatment. She never took chemotherapy or radiation. The cancer was clearly there in it's hideous form and then . . . it just wasn't there anymore. Medical records are available proving that something very extraordinary took place. Do I believe in miracles? No devil in the realms of Hell could ever convince me otherwise.

We were all witnesses to divine intervention when the doctor gathered us into that small back room, a quizzical look on his face, and cautiously announced that the cancer was no longer there. But we were to witness yet one more little reminder of God's grace the day we went to Jan's hospital room to take her home. My wife and I were gathering together her belongings and packing them into a small suitcase. Her nurse was there and we began to share with her our conviction that this was indeed a divine healing. Jan spoke up, "It was a miracle!" The nurse turned to her asking, "I'm sorry, did you ask me something?" It was then that I glanced down, for the first time, at the nurses name tag and suddenly chill waves rushed over my body. "Ma'am?" I asked the nurse whom we had only casually known as Debbie, "Is that really your last name?"

Until I breathe my final breath I shall always remember her answer as she looked at me and smiled, "Yes, I am Mrs. Miracle."

A Trip to Remember

I will never forget the day that most altered my life in a very strange and significant way. It is quite odd that I remember so vividly the date of October the tenth and yet I am unsure exactly what year it was. I do know it was the very early seventies, possibly nineteen seventy one, when I was around seventeen years old. The world was scented with the incense of rock and roll, mind expansion, and active rebellion over the war in Vietnam. When I should have been concerned about acne and dating problems I was instead anguishing over the paradoxes of life, nihilism, and transcendentalism. I was torn between eastern philosophies and the traditional ethics of the Appalachia foothills which had given rise to my very existence. No, the year did not seem important. But the cool crisp autumn breezes of October tenth and what took place that eventful day would never be erased from my memory. As a matter of fact it would forever alter my memory and concept of not only those early days but the majority of the years that followed.

The night before I had successfully slipped away from my parents home and thumbed to the little college town of Athens Ohio. Ohio University was a hippy haven nestled in the lush greenery of the great Ohio valley. Here, away from my parents watchful eyes, I could turn on, tune in, and drop out. My long hair and struggling beard hid the fact that I was just a teenager and I successfully merged in with the hip crowd drinking at the famed College Inn bar bathed in the purple haze of black lights and frenetic strobe pulsations. Somehow this wholly irreverent experience was a holy reverent experience in which we were the freaked out prophets shouting the apocalyptic message of love and peace as our only answer to survival. Over the blasting guitar strings of the Grateful Dead and the earthy wail of Bob Dylan's harmonica we shouted a quilted philosophy of eastern religion and Tim Leary-ism to the person sitting less then a foot in front of us. We touted great philosophical revelation and psychological concepts while chicks were whirling in ecstatic dance around us. We were the final revolutionaries. We were the prophets of the hour. We were pitifully drunk.

The frenzied night rolled endlessly on, producing profound insights that would never make sense in the morning. Finally the party was nearing the end. Happy hour was over. "Maggie" ended for the millionth time and the jukebox fell silent. The lights suddenly lit up the smoked filled room, causing our mysterious satori to vanish. The College Inn was closing. As we reluctantly stepped out of our mechanically induced magical mystery tour we stepped into the world of reality in which we had no way to get back to our boring little status seeking homes. As I discussed our minor dilemma with the buddies whom I had thumbed to Hippydom with, we were offered to stay at the college dorm with one of the heads we had been partying with that night.

The dorm was an upstairs nook complete with Spiritual Sky Krishna Consciousness incense hovering in the air, a door strung with Indian beads, and permeated with the holy anthems of the Beatles. Oh . . . and there were also some college text books stacked in a corner of the room for whatever reason. Our college friend slipped a dime bag of high quality pot out of his pocket and we proceeded to toke some holy sacrament. Confidentially I wasn't really interested in getting too religious on pot this hour of the morning. I was actually considering calling it a day. This was when the dorm guru brought out the ultimate sacrament . . . LSD. This was what I had been waiting for. I had read about it, heard about it, and sung about it, but this was the first time I was to ever actually be in the grand presence of it. It was a little orange pill christened as Orange Sunshine. I was warned that if I took it I would not sleep that night. I expressed my desire to sleep, so my dorm guru said he would wrap it up for me to take the next morning. It seems to me that it was a hit of three hundred micrograms of acid or possibly even a hit of six hundred micrograms. If I remember correctly he said he was giving me a quarter tab. To this day I doubt it was only a quarter tab due to the extraordinary results I was to experience. The little orange pill was wrapped up in a piece of cigarette package cellophane and I slipped it into my front pocket.

The next morning I woke up a bit queasy from the nectar of the gods I had drunk the night before. We had drunk our "soma" but for some reason I just didn't seem to feel immortal. We were alone in the sacred dorm. Our guru had apparently staggered off to class somewhere on campus.

We were walking down West Union Street near the campus when I remembered the little pill in my front pocket. I quickly searched for it and to my relief it was still there nestled between the cellophane covering of my filter tipped Tools and wrapped in its own little separate cocoon of cellophane the guru had carefully placed it in. I had been instructed to place the orange sacrament under my tongue for a more rapid absorption. This I did. It was a rather ordinary day that day. As a matter of fact it was actually a bland, boring, most uninteresting day. This was all about to be radically transformed.

We ran into some other teen age friends. My buddy John hooked up with his current girlfriend Jackie. We went to the little local hang out reminiscent of the restaurant seen on the Happy Days sit com. We sat in a booth near the door and started a bland little teen chat about insignificant matters. I glanced down at the table top in front of me. In the instant of that glance my whole world would dramatically change.

The table top came alive.

The table top was no longer a solid, nonliving, inanimate object. It was a thriving, living, pulsating act of creation.

Some years before I had seen a fresh blood sample under a high powered microscope and observed the living corpuscles as they flowed swiftly through self made canals. This table top had been artistically decorated with some sort of splotches. These little splotches were now flowing swiftly through self made canals just as beautifully and fluent as the blood corpuscles under the high powered microscope. The microscope was absent but there was certainly something "high powered" occurring. I gasped, "The table top is moving!! It looks like blood corpuscles flowing!!! LOOK . . . it's ALIVE!!"

This was the very first indication I had that I was affected in any way by the Lysergic Acid Diethylamide

The media had successfully persuaded a portion of my mind into expecting that a side effect of acid would possibly be insanity. I jumped to my feet, ran to the bathroom and proceeded to make myself regurgitate the drug I had never even swallowed in the first place. The toilet looked off center. I looked at myself in the mirror. My face looked off centered or subtly distorted in some way. I waited for my face to explode in an inferno of flames or for the flesh to melt from my scull as reported by the media. When it didn't happen I sighed with relief and realized I was probably going to be OK.

I returned to my friends who were totally freaked out. Their virgin brains had never lost it's mental innocence to the powerful deity of LSD. A little pot, beer, and some hyperventilation was as mind expanding as my teen peers had ventured into. They suggested we go for a walk down West Union Street. This little walk would culminate into one of the most incredible journeys of my lifetime.

It was a crisp autumn day. The air had a fresh scent to it.

John couldn't grow his hair long due to his compromising fear of rejection from the red neck crew he worked with back home. So when he came to Athens he donned a purple hat which sported a peace sign on the front of it. In his mind this transformed him into instant hip-ism. The autumn wind now caught his hat and it flew into the air as he raced after it. I glanced at it. Then I looked toward the sky. I noticed it's pure beauty. Then it happened.

The world which was covered by a bland and boring veneer was transformed as this veneer was suddenly and unexpectedly lifted. A great white light suddenly began to brighten everything before me and within me.

The only earthly example I can remotely compare it to was an experience I had as a child during a gloomy, cloudy day. A small rain had fallen. Without warning, the dark clouds gave way to the sunlight which immediately transformed the face of the planet. I stood in awe breathing in the fragrance after the rain.

For several years I had labored over which religion, which doctrine, or which teaching was true. I wanted to know the ultimate truth. Now here I was after ingesting this strange mystical substance called Orange Sunshine. As the covering of the world was lifted and the pure white light illuminated all, I suddenly realized *"THIS* is truth!"

I realized in that moment that truth was not a teaching, a doctrine, or a philosophy . . . Truth was an experience! There were no words for it. I was EXPERIENCING truth.

In my mind I believed I was experiencing God . . . not in the traditional way, but in some way unregulated by dogma.

The light was brilliant and vitally awesome, yet soft. It was cleansing and illuminating, it was alive and filled with wisdom and life — it was the pureness of all purity.

The bright light slowly diminished and left a pure world behind it. I could see the world for what it really was. Everything was washed in purity and I saw the world in it's sensitive, delicate reality. I could see the raw beauty of all before me. I saw the naked world. I saw it with ultra sensitive perception and it was beautiful . . . and I was part of it. I experienced my friends fear as well as their love and concern for me. I could "feel" with my eyes every sensitive expression on their faces. I could "feel" with my eyes everything around me. I experienced the dance of the autumn leaf that leaped and twirled in front of my path. Time slowed down until it was no more.

As I walked viewing the real world for the very first time the white light suddenly began to cause all to enlighten again. I had to immediately stop walking and once again bask in the great purity of truth, oneness, and cosmic consciousness.

Several times this great white light experience would appear, linger for blissful time, and then fade away again leaving a purified world behind it.

The doors of my perception had been cleansed. I was certain I had at long last discovered ultimate truth.

This was not the first mystical experience of total oneness and wonder I had ever had and neither was it to be the last. Prayer, meditation, sensory deprivation and other natural venues can allow one to be more receptive to "mystical experiences." However, this was the first time I not only *felt* the world dissolve but actually *saw* it dissolving with my own physical eyes! I not only *felt* the world was one, I was *seeing* it meld together before me! Certainly this was a spiritual epiphany differentiated only by the fact that I ingested a chemical instead of uttering a prayer. At least this is what I *thought*.

To understand how I came to revere this drug as a door to knowledge and spirituality I shall briefly present a few of the various and random theories I harbored concerning the effects of LSD upon the brain: According to psychologist William James the average person used only 10 percent of his brain. This left 90 percent of untapped brain potential. I believed that LSD opened up this 90 percent of the unused brain. I also believed that deep within the slumbering crypts of my genes and dormant brain cells was encoded information from all of my past ancestors . . . of the whole human race . . . of all creation from which we had evolved.

My brain was an unlimited library of billions of encyclopedic volumes. Did not even the birds inherit knowledge and instinct from their forebears such as how to build nests and which direction to fly for the winter? Has not every person at some time in their life experienced déjà vu, the experience that we have been at a certain place before and yet we know that in this lifetime we had never been to that particular place?

I was convinced that psychedelics such as LSD produced whole brain activation. Even as rich meaningful symbols surfaced in our dreams (which psychoanalysts claimed contained vital information about our inner selves) so too did deep rich meaningful symbols surface to the hallucinating mind. It was as if one opened the door to a cage of frightened birds which were suddenly allowed to soar free. My collective consciousness was tapped into and information came pouring forth. This brain that subconsciously absorbed information every moment of my existence (from its fetal stage in the womb to yesterdays subconscious absorption of subliminal messages which were encoded in the music at the Dentists office) was extracting answers to cosmic questions. My mind had access to the akashic records and the vibrational knowledge of the Universe. My brain was a cosmic computer, an ethereal library—a God machine.

My brain was meant to experience God. My bio-computer was hardwired for spiritual epiphanies. The chemical sacrament I had ingested had expanded my mind, cleansed my consciousness and activated the God centers in my brain. I could now tune in to the ultimate that surrounded me and and experience the absolute from which I came.

This was cosmic consciousness, enlightenment, unity consciousness, satori, nirvana, samadhi, chokma, illumination, and every ultimate spiritual and higher evolutionary experience all wrapped into one. I had arrived.

John took me to the upstairs pool room across the street. John was the nervous type and was quite sure I had been rendered irretrievably insane. He told me to lie down and rest after we got inside. I laid down and looked at the floor and SAW IT IN THREE DIMENSIONS! Today it is difficult to describe how one can view a flat surface object in three dimensions, but I can see it as clear today as I type these words as I did the day I experienced it. The texture and floral design of the floor somehow grew into a multidimensional object.

I closed my eyes and I instantly saw a long dark tunnel with a door at the end of it. The door unexpectedly open and a beautiful woman dressed in beautiful white flowing clothes swiftly drifted through the door. I reached out for her, sensing she was my long awaited soul mate, but she slipped from my reach and was gone. I opened my eyes.

I later closed my eyes again and found myself lying on an alter. The sun was shining brilliantly all around me and above me was a group of robed and hooded priests. For some reason I thought they were Aztec priests. I was the sacrifice on the alter. However I did not feel they were going to actually terminate my life but were in the sacred process of somehow elevating me to an office of priesthood and to a higher spiritual consciousness.

Some dude in charge of the pool hall came over and asked John what was wrong with me. John, afraid to tell him I had been made irreversibly insane by LSD, instead told him I was drunk. The dude then told John if I was going to stay there I would have to set up and not lie down on the floor.

I believe I was wearing a purple shirt with the huge belled sleeves with a green vest over it. The vest had been an army jacket from Nam. The sleeves were torn off from it and there had been a USA flag sown upside down on the back of it. An irate teacher at school had confiscated the jacket and ripped off the flag before returning the vest to me. That was the beginning of quite a riot at our school. I loved it! (In retrospect, although not really certain, I do believe this occurred prior to my cosmic trip). The threads of that ripped off flag still clung to the vest as a reminder that I was a soldier in the revolutionary army of the deranged youth of America (Although against the war in Vietnam I was not among those who downgraded our soldiers. This was not their war. I felt respect for their courage and great sadness that they were being exploited by a corrupt government. They were just kids . . . like myself. It was the corruptness of the government that I loathed and was rebelling against). I was wearing faded bell bottomed blue jeans with leather sewn in the side of the bells. I wore an Egyptian ankh around my neck. My hair was long and was now falling in front of my bearded face. I don't think I had my Billy Jack hat, with the peacock feather in it, with me that day.

John came over and told me I had to sit up. The media had saturated our schools with LSD horror stories and a couple of these floated up to consciousness. We had been incorrectly informed that LSD could cause chromosomal damage and when this forgotten bit of information bobbed to the surface I thought I could faintly feel and hear the chromosomes crackling and breaking. I suddenly remembered the story about someone that took LSD and thought he was exploding into flames. They took him screaming in terror to the mental hospital. I started feeling very uncomfortably warm. I looked for the tell tale signs of smoke and braced myself for the explosion. When it didn't happen I sighed with relief.

The walls waved and moved like ocean water. Solid surfaces had the buoyancy of a water bed.

I looked at my hand and for the first time I could see it in it's true reality . . . with full "sensitivity" . . . without the "veneer."

I saw John's girlfriend Jackie asking him something. Most considered Jackie beautiful enough to have been a model. She was slender and simply oozed with femininity. Her eyes were a timid sky blue and sparkled in a shy way. Her skin was soft and satin smooth, perfect without blemish. The most remarkable feature about her was her flowing silky blonde hair. It seemed florescent at times. When she walked into a room everything would stop and all eyes would revert to her. She usually wore light colors and this day she was wearing a white one piece mini skirt. One thing that really puzzled me was why in the world she was with John. He was no where near her league. I guess I didn't have to know Jackie long to discover why she was with John. She was with him but for a very short stint. Then she was with someone else . . . and then with someone else . . . and then with someone else . . . and then with . . . oh well, you get the picture. Today some would call her a name fashioned after a gardening implement. I won't tell you whether that implement is a rake or a hoe but I think you can read between the lines. She had a reputation.

Jackie asked John if she could help me. Compassion flowed from her asking eyes. John told her yes. She came over and sat on my lap. She looked deep into my eyes. Seductively she slipped her warm arms around my neck. Her luminescent hair brushed across my cheek. Her soft embrace held me close in her attempt to comfort me. I could smell her make up and perfume. I could sense her passion. I was in the embrace of a gardening implement that had a loose reputation with everyone in town, *however,* I could not shake the feeling that she was a pure, unspotted virgin goddess. She was a female deity. Almost like a virgin Mary. It made no difference how many or who she indifferently slept with or that she was the epitome of the sexual revolution, I was convinced this was the holiest of virgins.

I never slept around like my buddies did. And there was no temptation on this very exceptional day in the pool hall — especially not with deity. All I could see, think, or experience was this spiritual satori. This experience seemed to elevate us so far above ordinary, mundane material life that before the day was over we would *all* seem to become some sort of "deity."

We later we walked down Court Street to Arthur Treacher's Restaurant. This was really our main hang out. In the past it was the Rainbow Restaurant and it was here that my father and mother first met. It was also here I had bought the first Pepsi for the first girl I ever got up nerve enough to talk to. It was here my brain burst into a universe of multicolored images. I lay my head down on the table and I saw the most remarkable maze of intricate images . . . the most complex array of patterns and colors. When my friends wanted to leave I reluctantly came out of orbit. I wanted to experience more. The waiter of the store went to my high school and was a bona fide red necked square — a pompous overbearing bona fide red necked square. He peered over the counter and grinned this snarling grin at me and said, "He's high on somethin' ain't he?" I replied, "Yeah . . . on acid , man. Like, wow . . . I just saw a building walking down the street." I had seen no such thing but that statement would later enter into the urban legends of our high school as a fact.

I tried to enter some deep philosophical and religious conversation with my friends but either I was too deep for them or I was too incoherent. It was hard to tell the difference. I'm not sure there was a difference.

We went to the children's home which was located in Athens. We knew several teenage girls that were temporarily living there. I remember looking at the green leaves of the tree's around the building. They somehow looked very different than before. My long time friend Jeanie came out of the house and embraced me. She laughed when she saw how high I was. We talked awhile. She comforted me with her words and then asked me if I would ever turn my life over to the Lord. The dorm mother of the home came out. She had been one of the dedicated saints at the church I used to frequent. She walked toward me and fixed her eyes of compassion deeply onto mine. She began to witness to me of the love of Christ. Although I had been in church before, I didn't have the full revelation of truth. As I began to listen to the dorm mother exalt the love of Christ and his sacrifice for me, something began to seem different. All of a sudden this great experience of cosmic consciousness and ultimate enlightenment paled dimly in the light of Christ's love. It seemed so insignificant and selfish. It seemed as though all I was now experiencing was mental hallucination via a foreign chemical.

A lot of grand experiences no doubt took place that day in my mind but has since been laid to rest with the various brain cells I have sloughed off with other chemicals and drink. I recall that right after my trip I filled a couple of pages with reminders of things I had experienced in my cosmic journey. I only wrote a sentence or a word as a title to remind me of a certain experience and then under that I would write another word or sentence about another experience I'd had that day and then another under that title, etc, until the page was full. I had the intention of going back later and expounding on each of those experiences in full. Not only have I lost that list but I must have forgotten quite a bit because I can no longer make such an extensive list about that particular trip as I did back then. Today I remember only the highlights. Some of those highlights I wished I could forget . . . which brings me back to the story.

We ended up in a residential area of Athens where Jackie lived. John told me to wait outside while he and Jackie shared some private time inside. It was dark by now and I was still tripping heavily. John pried open Jackie's bedroom widow and very quietly began to climb inside trying not to awaken Jackie's father who was sound asleep in his own bedroom at the other end of the house. Jackie slipped in behind him. It was a tense enough situation knowing that if Jackie's father woke up that we could be facing the fury of an angry man, who just may also possess a shotgun, but I also was aware that it was night and my own father who was an anti-drug, anti-hippy, and anti-Curtis-my-rebellious-son type of personality was probably loading his own shotgun about this time. I sat quietly on the front porch swing waiting for John and allowed my eyes to take in the strangely quiet neighborhood. This was the first time I had been really been left alone since the beginning of my chemical journey. It was an uneasy situation. Little did I know it at that time but my euphoric, enlightening, Heaven on earth was about to bottom out as I was about to plunge suddenly and uncontrollably into the tormenting hands of the demons of Hell.

I closed my eyes perhaps thinking I would go back to my little world of complex patterns and colors. Instead I found myself back in the College Inn, the bar where this all began. It was as though I was actually there. I saw black lights, flashing strobes, and a group of hippys dancing as one pulsating body. Out of the crowd an unknown hipster with wooly hair, frizzy beard, gaping mouth and wild demon possessed eyes suddenly lunged forward, directly into my face. Startled my eyes flew open! Wow . . . how weird. I closed my eyes and there he was again trying to attack me.

Just when I decided it was safer to keep my mind on the real world . . . the real world began to go crazy. Around the corner spun my fathers car and he slammed on the brakes, leaned out the window and started screaming at me. "Just what in the world do you think you're doing!! You just decide not to come home last night? I am gonna beat you until you can't walk straight!!!" I quietly arose from the porch swing and started toward the car. "Your drunk!" he screamed. I got in the back seat of his car as he continued an avalanche of screams that suddenly had no meaning. It was the "Wha-Wha-Wha" of Charlie Browns cartoon parents. It was then that I looked down on the floorboard of the car and there were several dead bodies that were crammed in there. These were bodies of the undead. I looked down at these living dead creatures and smiled at them . . . we had a secret. My father thought I was drunk but *WE* knew better. I felt no fear, anger, nor anything else toward my Dad. I was even smug in my secret.

Unpredictably when we got out of the car and entered the house he told me we would take care of this situation the next morning. Dad then went upstairs to go to bed. I walked over to the sandwich bar in the kitchen and my mother came in asking me if I was alright, did I get into any trouble, had I been drinking, she had been worried about me, etc. She finally got around to asking me if I was hungry. In retrospect I don't think that I had eaten nor had any appetite the entire day. It suddenly occurred to me since all my senses had been so super sensitized and magnified that eating should result in an exploding, unbelievable taste experience. Mom asked what I wanted . . . did I want a sandwich . . . did I want lettuce . . . did I want mayonnaise? Yes, yes, yes! I was ready to enter the mystical world of lavish, sensual taste and splendor! I took a bite of the sandwich . . . it tasted like cardboard and stale bread. I looked at it . . . the lettuce appeared to be old and wilted. When I commented on this, my mother protested in surprise that it was absolutely fresh. I could not eat it. Food seemed foreign to me. Taste was bland, lifeless, and a worthless habit to revery in. It just didn't seem to belong in my mouth. So much for gourmet mysticism.

After everyone had finally retired for the evening I was sitting in the semi-darkness of the kitchen. I rose to go to the bathroom, walking through the dark hall between the kitchen and lavatory.

I need to pause at this point of the story and press the rewind button back to an incident I'd had years ago while very young. There was an old hermit that lived in a run down shack near our house. There was no bathroom or running water in his shack. The hermit, whose name was Fred, was a severe alcoholic. He was a rather tall man with long sad, almost scary features. He had haunting eyes, gray hair, and had a stiff Herman Munster kind of walk. I was never really afraid of him. Despite his strange cryptic lifestyle he treated all of the children in the village with kindness. One day he made his stiff Herman Munster walk out to his front porch and called my name. He said he would give me twenty five cents if I brought him up three or four jugs of water every week. WOW! Twenty five cents to a twelve year old seemed like a great entrepreneurial move. So each week I brought his jugs of water. I would knock on his rickety door and listen as he dragged himself out of his dilapidated broken down armchair, which he had retrieved from the local dump, and stiff leggedly made his way to the door to see who was bothering him. As the faded and pealing green door slowly cracked open, all I could see inside was blackness. Then his pale white face, smudged with coal soot, appeared as he cautiously peered through the crack. He would extend a long gangly arm and in his gnarled hands was a quarter. I would give him his jugs of water and then scurry off with my treasure.

One cold winter day I knocked on his door and there was no answer. I set the jugs in front of his door and went home. The following week when I came to his house I was surprised to see last weeks water jugs still there . . . frozen and busted. Quizzically I wiped the dirt from his cracked window and peered inside his insidious nook and saw him lying on the floor. I knew there was a problem. I directed my shoulder toward the door lunging toward it and breaking the frail lock on the other side. As the door swung open I could see the warped walls covered in black coal soot that had accumulated from years of using the coal stove for heat. I immediately noticed there was no heat in the room. He was lying on the floor with his hand reaching out toward the coal stove. I ran to him and grasped his shoulder . . . he was frozen solid!

When the coroner arrived, according to my Father the village storyteller, they had to break Fred's frozen arm in order to get him out of the door. It was believed that as he sat in his chair, drunk on Thunderbird wine, that he let the fire go out. He then struggled to get to the coal stove in order to shake the grate and revive the fire, but he died with his hand reaching out just inches from the stoves grate. Quite a discovery for a young kid to make.

Fast forward now back to my memorable trip.

Here I am sitting in the kitchen. I rise to go to the bathroom walking through the dark hall between the kitchen and lavatory. I put my hand on the bathroom doorknob, open it up, and to my utter horror standing in front of me with threatening outstretched arms is . . .

. . . Fred!!!

I froze.

His eyes were bulging and menacing. His long gangly

Herman Munster arms were high over his head. His mouth was aggressively gaped wide open, his teeth were glaring in the darkness—he was ready to attack.

He was there.

I saw him.

Just as plainly as I used to see him as a child he was there.

And he didn't seem too happy that I'd let his water jugs freeze.

It never occurred to me this might be a hallucination. For some odd reason my reason was oddly not working.

Every hair on my body stood on end. My legs refused to move. I was stunned . . . shocked . . . horrified. There are no words that can describe the sheer terror I felt! Every cell in my body was electrified with total overcoming fear!

This was a prime heart attack moment.

Suddenly I turned and ran for my life.

My mother had some problems sleeping upstairs in her bedroom and was sleeping on the couch.

Our house was heated by fuel oil and she said it got too cold upstairs. I'm not sure if she was referring to the temperature of her marriage or the house but we never questioned her.

I woke her up and told her I could not sleep upstairs in my own room this night. I asked if I could sleep in the chair near her. She got up and put two easy chairs facing each other which resulted in a nice little nest to land in. From that night forward, until I came to the fullness of truth, I was to never again sleep in my bedroom or any room by myself nor was I able to sleep without a light on in the room. Mom went back to her couch and I lay on mine with a million philosophical and religious ideas running through my head.

I closed my eyes and I saw the whole earth . . . the whole

universe. It was as though I was lifted high above earth and was observing all of the trees and all of the people on the planet. Suddenly out of nowhere came a rich flowing baptism of overwhelming love.

It was not a love for a particular person or thing but just love for love's sake.

Remember how you felt when you first fell madly in love with someone of the opposite sex? Remember how you saw stars, your heart pounded, and you were lost in a dream cloud of ecstasy? Take that feeling and multiply it a million times and you will begin to understand just a little of the great experience of love I was experiencing. I was so flooded with love that my heart began to beat so hard I thought it would come out of my chest. I could feel it pounding with passion against my ribs like a bird against it's cage seeking to soar into the sky. Overwhelming love . . . ecstatic love . . . unbelievable, overpowering, all encompassing, totally permeating, indescribable love!

It bathed every cell in my body. It consumed me. It overpowered me. It possessed me. Love rolled over and over and over again throughout my whole being. It burst in me . . . flowed in me . . . became me. There was nothing but total consuming love!

This experience lasted for what seemed like forever. It was as though it would never or could never end. Somehow I finally drifted off to sleep.

Who knows what frontiers I may have trod in my dreams that night.

The next morning things seemed fresh. I was not seeing things but I still felt high. It seemed I felt a bit high the whole day. Later that night a friend of mine came over and I looked toward the hills and was sure I had seen a red light appear. As a child I believed in UFO's and was sure they were landing on that hill. Now I had some visual proof. "Look . . . there it is again!" I shouted, scaring my friend Roy half to death. "Where, where?"

he anxiously asked. "There, there it is again!" I exclaimed. He told me later that I was really freaking him out.

I later sat down and thoughtfully pondered over each and every experience I'd had that crisp day in October. I wasn't sure the ecstasy was worth the terror so it would be awhile before I got high on LSD again. From that day forward I never slept in a room by myself nor would I sleep in darkness without a light on. I was afraid that Fred would come back. There were other trips that I eventually embarked upon and other spiritual experiences I delved into, but I was to never fully shake either the ecstasy nor the horror of that crisp autumn day. Sometimes I would thumb home from Athens and it would get dark, or I would have to go to the barn to check on the animals at night, and the fear and distress would return. In a panic I would frantically recite the 23rd Psalm "Yea though I walk through the valley of the shadow of death . . ."

I knew that valley.

And Fred was in it waiting on me.

It wasn't until I came to the Church and received the Lord in my life that I was able to again sleep in a room by myself or to sleep in darkness.

When chemically induced satori failed to give direction to my life or to quench the thirsting of my inner spirit I ultimately returned to the God of my childhood. I came to the realization that I had been very deceived by an artificial experience and that it was but a pale imitation of a real spiritual encounter with the living God. Little did I realize God would one day use me to reach countless hundreds of others who were in the very condition that I had been in.

The adventure seemed long and arduous. I had come to the conclusion that it took far more incredulous faith to believe this world is an accident than it did to believe that a creator had created it. The marvel of irreducible complexity and the breathtaking beauty of harmonious design demanded an intelligent designer. The very eyes by which I view this living world around me seemed so magnificently made that to construe them as the result of a series of accidents would be the epitome of gullible faith. There was much more behind existence than random circumstance. There was intelligence in the universe. There was a higher power.

Many religions were existent in the world and I had experimented with all of them — or at least as many of them as was possible. Each religion had a god and each god allegedly inspired a "bible" or a book of some sort. To discover which god was the right God I searched the "bible" each god had inspired to be written. While some of these writings were fantastic legends that included such tales as the earth being a flat square sitting on the top of a turtle in a huge ocean which was floating on top of another turtle that was on top of another turtle, ad infinitum, I saw in the Holy Bible of the Judaic-Christian world a sensible story of a God that created all things. This book stated that God hung the circle of the earth upon nothing. I read of events this Bible had prophesied of that had truly come to pass. I read of archaeological finds that substantiated biblical history.

But more than all this . . . I was experiencing a God in my heart that really cared about me . . . and I hadn't consumed a chemical to experience him.

I went to the altar that night, and that night completely altered my life.

It was a dramatically life transforming experience. The overwhelming love of Christ that saturated my being was much greater than the artificial ecstasy induced by a chemical. I had a personal experience with a personal savior and that was an experience the adversary could never duplicate.

It was but a few months later I had a road to Damascus experience — I saw the glory and the light of God. It bore no resemblance to the light I experienced while tripping. It was real. It was more magnificent. It was *personal*. It wasn't merely the atmosphere lighting up — I actually beheld the glorious light appear in a cloud of shining brilliance before me. It reached out to me, touched me, and permeated me with a genuine cleansing holiness and godly awe. This was the truth I had searched for. I would never be the same again.

My old friends were stunned by my sudden transformation. Some of them were angered by it. Many of them were moved by it and and ultimately gave their lives to Jesus Christ.

The sojourn was rugged, but I found my way.

Sometimes when my life seems lonely and I doubt my purpose . . . I remember my journey. I remember my frantic search for truth.

And I remember Fred.

I remember how my anguished search for meaning led me to the faith I personally embrace today and my firm belief that it will one day take me to my eternal home . . . and that will be a trip to remember.

Yesterday

I had climbed the small hill as far as my exhausted legs would take me. I turned and sat down on it's grassy slopes as my eyes scanned the panoramic view of the quaint little village below me. A sweet tender breeze washed my senses in honeysuckle while a robin in the big oak tree serenaded me. I had struggled up this hill for no other reason than just to be be here and do exactly what I wasn't doing and not having to answer to anyone for not doing it. I was king of the world. Time stood still.

I could see the little country church to my right and the old railroad depot to my left. The little village was separated by a railroad track that went through it. Except for the rare roar of the trains mighty whistle and the occasional barking of a lonely dog, things were usually very quiet and serene in Mineral. The little houses were lined up along the road separated by a few friendly trees. To my far left was the old store building and in front of it was the old bridge. The laughter of children suddenly filled the air as they chased a barking little puppy up and down the road. The puppy would flee from them, then suddenly turn around and begin to chase the children as they squealed with glee. I heard a mother's voice call out, probably calling them in for lunch or telling them to get off the hard road.

Behind me was an enchanted woods filled with ginseng and hickory nut trees. The rare glimpse of a squirrel's sleek body as it disappeared into the brush reminded me of the world teaming with life beneath it's wooded grove. They too had their own little village of sorts.

Startled I suddenly wake up out of my sleep to the sound of hurried traffic impatiently racing to work and the almost sonic sounding boom of an eighteen wheeler tanking by. I rise from my bed with a sigh. I throw on my kimono and hurry to the kitchen, grab myself a glass of chlorinated water and glancing at the clock I realize I am late. I should be in the midst of that rambling traffic by now. I suddenly realize the grassy hill, the panoramic view of the little village, and the laughter of frolicking children was just a dream . . . a dream that came to me in the wee hours of the night, reminding me of a little village called Mineral Ohio . . . a place where I grew up and learned that the most important things in life was life itself. I shrug and run my fingers through my tangled hair. It was just a dream. But as I look out the window at the smog that is slowly giving way to a few struggling beams of sunlight, I wonder. I wonder between the dream and the waking which is the dream and which is the reality. I really wonder.

(Originally written in 1998)

Observing an Orange

I picked up an orange and it was cool to the touch. Looking closely at its texture I could see the hundreds of little hills and valleys connecting themselves in perfect orange array. Scraping my fingernail across its surface produced a light spray of fresh citrus that burst forth like a tiny orange fountain. Suddenly the air is filled with the most delightful scent. There are little cells in the peel filled with orange oil that when released are much more fragrant than the fruit it covers. While most people slice an orange in half, I personally like to peel it with my fingers. My mother used to tell me that oranges never smelled so good as when I ate them. It was some time before I realized I was producing an effervescent shower of orange oil each time I peeled one.

As I open the fruit, little streams of juice spill out onto my hand and then onto the table. I close my eyes and taste its nectar realizing that in some third world countries this would be an experience to almost die for. As I mull a juicy bite with my tongue I can now feel an almost foreign object in my mouth. It is a seed. As I look at the small white seed I realize I am looking at a small miracle. Within this seed is the genetic blueprint for a whole new orange tree. Within lies the potential of a whole orchard and generations of future orchards. Looking at the other seeds still embedded in the fruit I realize that while I can count the seeds in this orange, only God can count the oranges in the seed.

A Drive Through the City

My wife and I went for a relaxing drive and slowed down a bit to admire a piece of property adorned by natural landscape. It seemed to stand out oddly in the midst of this asphalt jungle we call the city. We were suddenly aware of an adrenaline surge behind us as a red faced driver shook his tight fist and waved his fat little arm at us. He began to sound his horn as a progression of red faced, tight fisted, fat armed people lined up behind him. He stuck a stubby finger up at us as he angrily chewed on his cigar burping out words we did not care to lipread. My wife, who was driving, pushed the accelerator and, with an extra puff of carbon monoxide released into the atmosphere, we were on our way.

A few miles closer to home we weaved in and out of a maze of traffic and shot into the McDonald's entrance. Our pressured day, now far spent, granted us a few minutes to order a couple of hamburgers drenched in saturated fat topped with pickles containing green dye, some greasy french fries, and a carbonated sugary drink that resembles absolute nothing in nature. Refueled we rushed on home just in time for the kids to get home from school. I sighed a deep breath of stale city air and unlocked my padlocked door to let my family in. My son flips on our 42 inch color television just in time to hear a news bulletin describing a murder that had taken place earlier that day. "I'm so glad we live in a good neighborhood," my wife exclaimed as she reset the burglar alarm. My son pointed the multifunctional remote control toward the television and with the push of a finger the bulletin was gone. In it's place was a politician extolling the virtues of modern progress and how, by raising tax dollars, we can expedite modern progress in our grand city.

The chemicalized, mechanically ruled, concrete world we were living in was a far cry from the real world in which I was reared. I refer to it as the real world because fresh air, pure streams of water, and lush greenery was the original state in which the world was created. It was a world in which you actually knew your neighbors and if you were stranded along a road somewhere people actually stopped to lend a hand instead of pulling out a gun and shooting you.

Sometimes I go back to the old homestead where I was raised and I marvel. I walk through the woods and listen to the silent messages being spoken to me.

Although we lived awhile in the city I eventually moved my family and I into a nice rural area just a heartbeat away from the real country. For awhile the family suffered from carbon monoxide withdrawal but they adjusted just fine.

If you have no idea what I am talking about, you need to take a long relaxing drive through the city and think about it. And while you're stopped at the red light, tell the red face, tight fisted driver with the stubby finger that we don't really miss him and if we can help it we will not be seeing him any time soon . . . not anytime soon at all.

(Originally written in 1998)

True Love

The first time I set my eyes on Rebecca I knew I had fallen madly in love with her. But falling in love is like enjoying the vivid colors and the tantalizing scent of a beautiful flower—if you pick it for that reason alone the flower will wilt and die. True respect for the flower demands you allow it to take root and to grow. After initially *falling* in love I learned to *grow* in love.

I fell in love with a young girl whose long lush hair flowed in breathtaking waves over her back. I have grown to love a woman whose every occasional gray hair is a testament to the struggles we have weathered together on the journey that we call life.

I fell in love with a young lass whose lipid blue eyes caused me to dissolve by simply looking into mine. I have grown to love a woman whose eyes can relay a message to me without her ever speaking a word—such as "It's OK darling, I know what your going through right now and I am with you every step of the way."

I fell in love with a sixteen year old that made my heart flutter uncontrollably when she touched her hand to mine. I have grown to love a faithful wife who, sensing when I am discouraged, simply places her hand on my shoulder, assuring me that I am not alone in my trial.

I fell in love with a perfect angel who thought I was a perfect knight in shining armor. I have grown in love with an angel who learned to love me through my imperfections and I through hers.

From time to time we still fall madly in love with each other all over again. We don't fall in love when facing a financial crunch. We aren't falling in love when death comes to a friend or loved one. We aren't seeing romantic fireworks when sickness strikes our home—but we are *growing* in love each and every step of life that we experience together.

Falling in love is beautiful. It still happens to us. But every single day we open our eyes, every breath we breath, and every new crisis we weather, we are growing in love. We are growing stronger in the reassurance that we will always be there for each other. We are growing stronger in our respect and admiration for each other.

I thank the Lord over and over for the beautiful little rose I saw that day in nineteen seventy five. But I thank him even more for the beautiful little rose with whom I was privileged to set my roots next to, allowing us to grow together.

Falling in love was wonderful.

Growing in love has been sacred.

Finis

Copyright © 2010 Curtis D. Ward

All rights reserved.

Revision 8

AtriaBookPublishing@gmail.com

Author contact information can be forwarded by writing the publisher at the email address above. Please type "Author contact request: Curtis Ward" in the subject heading.

www.ingramcontent.com/pod-product-compliance
Lightning Source LLC
Chambersburg PA
CBHW020010050426
42450CB00005B/407